Photographers Credits

All color slides and chromes were taken by
Fred George, Fred George Photography,
Ken Dean

All before and during construction shots were taken by
BRB Staff Members

The aerial shots of the piers before construction were taken by
Beck's Studio

Computer rendering of Chelsea Piers management offices by
BRB Staff Members, John Knoetgen, Project Architect
at Butler Rogers Baskett

Black and white headshots of partners were taken by
Scott Stembach

Editorial Director USA
Pierantonio Giacoppo

Chief Editor of Collection
Maurizio Vitta

Publishing Coordinator
Franca Rottola

Graphic Design
Paola Polastri

Editing
Jesse Oona Nickerson
Martyn J. Anderson

Color-separation
Litofilms Italia, Bergamo

Printing
Poligrafiche Bolis, Bergamo

First published March 1997

ISBN 88-7838-024-5

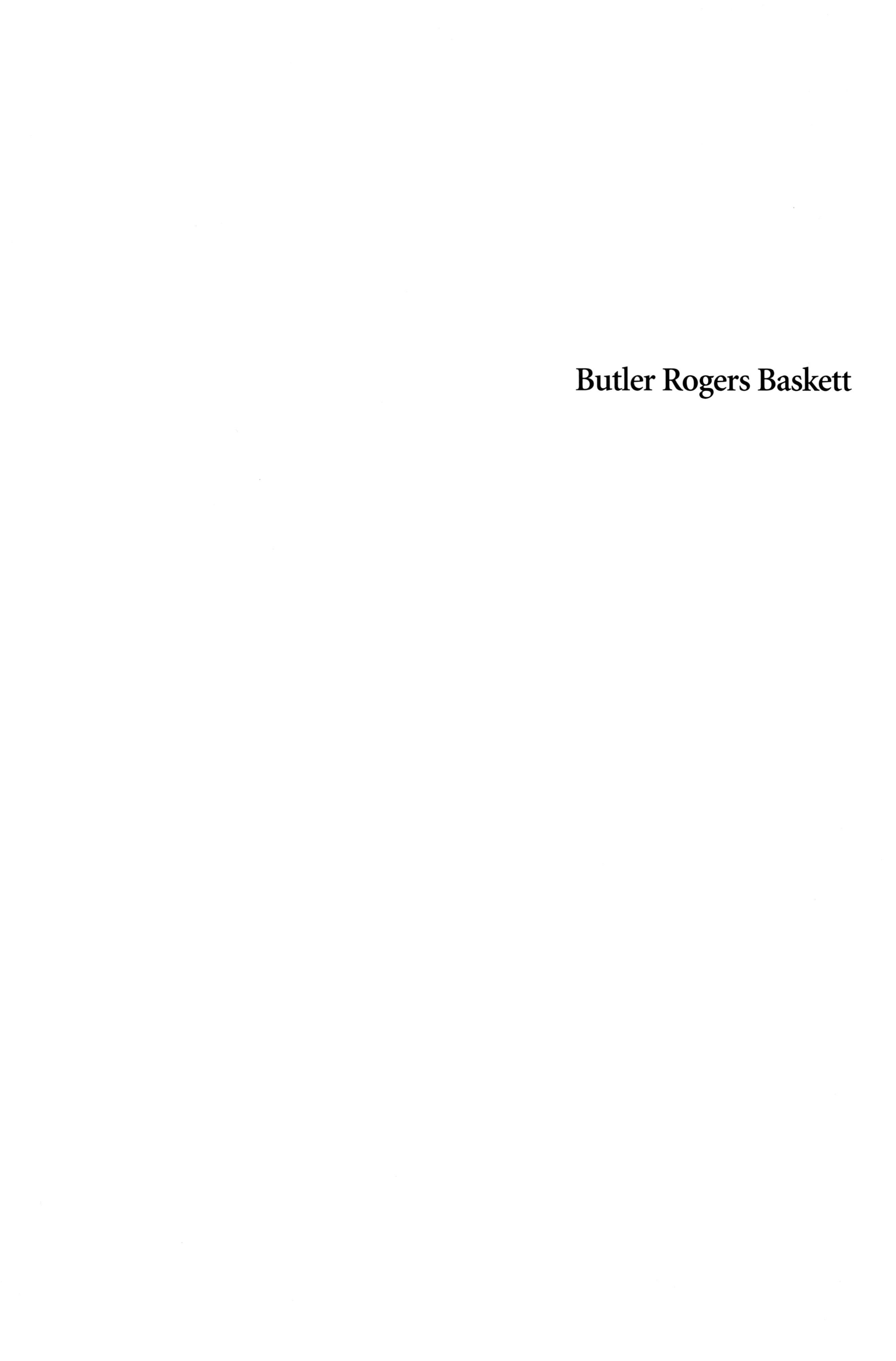

Butler Rogers Baskett

Butler Rogers Baskett
Revitalizing the Waterfront

Text by
Anthony Iannacci

Introduction by
James G. Rogers, III, FAIA

Contents

New Life for New York City

by James G. Rogers, III, FAIA

Sometimes careful preparation and planning are the keys to success. At other times, it is a willingness to seize unexpected opportunities and to boldly pursue what conventional wisdom suggests cannot be accomplished.

The evolution of the Chelsea Piers Sports and Entertainment Complex is the story of just such an opportunity seized, and of what grew into an unwavering commitment to prove that four, nearly derelict, piers on the Hudson River could become once again a vibrant part of the life of New York City.

The story begins with the figure-skating career of Jessie Betts, the teenaged daughter of film executive Roland Betts, who took ice-skating lessons along with many other enthusiastic young skaters at Manhattan's only indoor public facility, Sky Rink.

It was, unfortunately yet understandably, located on the roof of a building located at 44th Street and 10th Avenue. It was unfortunate, because of its inaccessibility; and understandable, because ice-skating rinks require some 20,000 square feet of unobstructed space, and city rooftops are among the few spaces which meet this requirement.

Betts, also a hockey enthusiast, subsequently became involved in the operation of Sky Rink and, recognizing the limitations of the location, he soon began looking for a new site.

In addition to rooftops, of course, pier sheds meet a skating rink's requirements for unobstructed space; and Pier 61 at 23rd Street and the Hudson River soon became the object of interest for Betts and his partners, Tom Bernstein and David Tewksbury.

Pier 61 is part of a complex of buildings stretching from 17th Street to 23rd Street encompassing some 1.2 million square feet. These buildings are an important part of New York's rich and varied maritime history, though ultimately, it was the decline of New York as a port which led to their availability for other uses.

The piers were designed by Warren and Wetmore (the firm which designed Grand Central Station) and built in 1912. But as the era of grand ocean travel began to decline in the mid-20th century, new uses were sought for these structures. New York City was still a busy port and it was believed that the piers could be renovated and made into the centerpiece of a growing cargo trade.

The renovation was completed in the early 1960s, but the cargo trade never materialized. Thus in 1992, when Betts and his partners went looking for a site for Sky Rink, they found at Chelsea Piers—Piers 59 through 62 and the connecting Headhouse—a site which had been structurally refurbished but was being only marginally used.

Betts immediately asked us, at Butler Rogers Baskett, to evaluate the feasibility of placing Sky Rink on Pier 61. We quickly learned that

New York State, owner of the pier complex, required the entire 1.2 million-square-foot complex, not just a single pier, to be rented, and that it could only be rented to private interests through a public auction.

This set in motion the process of determining what other activities could be added to the two ice-skating rinks already planned for Pier 61 in order to make the whole a thriving, exciting, and most importantly, economically viable development.

Betts and his partners were the winning bidders at the auction, and after four years of extraordinarily fast-paced planning, approval, and execution, the Chelsea Piers Sports and Entertainment Complex, including the ice-skating rinks, is now complete with a staggering list of adjoining activities.

We are proud to have been involved with such a project that focuses on the recreational needs of children at a time when other resources are diminishing. We are also happy to observe that our work has become a catalyst for other development in the community.

The Chelsea Piers Sports and Entertainment Complex revitalizes an important part of the New York City waterfront unlike any other project. It has restored confidence in the viable success of commercial development of outdated, abandoned urban infrastructures, and has directly influenced the formation of other such projects.

An Oasis of Urban Relief

by Anthony Iannacci

Most New Yorkers maintain the notion that their city is a difficult place to live and that it offers little escape from the downside of hyper-urban existence.

Notwithstanding its status as a private venture, the Chelsea Piers Sports and Entertainment Complex is a milestone in the revitalization of New York City's waterfront and recreational facilities. Together with private development, the Butler Rogers Baskett architects and designers have created a facility that provides New Yorkers with a rare opportunity to enjoy the Hudson River.

For years the City and State of New York have tried to invigorate Manhattan's Hudson River waterfront without great success.

The impasse was largely due to the fact that environmentalists, community boards, and State and City residents could not collectively focus their energies on a single project. Federal funds were earmarked for the construction of Westway, a major interstate highway, but city residents rightfully wanted more from their federal funding than a highway they perceived as being for non-New Yorkers.

While the debate over what to do with the West Side continued, many of the piers disintegrated into dangerous wreckage.

The Chelsea Piers Project demonstrates that the abandoned structures along the waterfront can be reincarnated without the sort of start-from-scratch mentality associated with earlier proposals.

The project also illustrates that the needs of the community can, in part, be met by a partnership between commercial development and good design. According to the Westway proposal, the remains of the Chelsea Piers were to have been demolished, but this project was canceled in 1985. By 1990, a new proposal by the West Side Waterfront Panel earmarked the Chelsea Piers as the potential site of some 720,000 square feet of residential space and 110,000 square feet of commercial space.

In 1992, while waiting for such a project to become economically feasible, the State Transportation Department decided to search for an interim tenant for the piers.

Which is when the partnership Chelsea Piers L. P. (composed of Betts, Bernstein, and Tewksbury) decided to develop a sports facility on the site.

Butler Rogers Baskett's experience with historic preservation and the design of gyms, schools, and recreational facilities provided them with the unique experience required to marry the proposed program with the architectural and historic integrity of the piers.

In order to meet New York City approval requirements, the architects were driven through an unprecedented and complex process. The proposal involved the most comprehensive series of variances in the history of the city.

The piers, which are on the New York City waterfront but are owned by the State of New York, were privately leased, and this particular situation required that the architects obtain a special zoning designation.

To further complicate matters, the buildings existed for 85 years without having a certificate of occupancy, and therefore, there were

In 1963 the original cast-concrete arches were removed from the east-facing facade when the piers were renovated for use as a cargo terminal. The facade was then replaced by a low-maintenance, banal metal wall. Today the eastern facade, as seen here from across the West Side Highway, hosts billboard-type images along with a series of signs and graphics indicating the different venues within.

no up-to-date construction regulations or zoning requirements dealing with life safety or public access for pier designs.

The decrepit and decaying structures had also been designated by the National Register of Historic Places, and the architects had to comply with Landmark guidelines.

In addition to these concerns, the architects discovered that the underwater structures required extensive maintenance, and due to the size and proposed change in use of the piers the project required a full, environmental impact statement.

Butler Rogers Baskett prepared the necessary drawings and documents for the various approval processes and later created a design that conformed with the various building, traffic, and environmental requirements.

In doing so, the architects set a highly innovative and creative precedent for the adaptive reuse of urban infrastructures, which would not only have a positive affect on the community, but also on the environment.

Between 25 and 30 million dollars were spent on infrastructure alone: electrical service, plumbing, water and sewer lines, sprinkler, fire alarms, and emergency lighting. Since each venue required a unique environmental solution—temperatures ranging from 50 degrees for year-round ice-skating rinks to 80 degrees for the swimming pool to heated outdoor golf stalls—the design of the mechanical and electrical systems for the project represented a major challenge for the architects and the project engineers, Cosentini Associates.

The four 880-foot piers and the 90,000 square-foot Headhouse were renovated to host a variety of both public and private facilities. The complete project reclaimed the unused and decaying waterfront structures while providing unrestricted public access to the waterfront in the form of a 20 foot-wide, 1.2 mile-long esplanade that runs along the perimeter of each of the piers.

The Butler Rogers Baskett architects held the disparate uses of the entire complex together with bold and colorful graphics, large-scale geometry and simple detailing, and materials that were to become important architectural themes. The Chelsea Piers Sports and Entertainment Complex was clearly designed to convey a message of energy, movement, fun, and physical activity.

Until recently New York seemed to maintain a distant relationship to both its waterfront and its historical position as a port city.

Most New Yorkers today have actually never departed from Manhattan by boat. The Chelsea Piers Sports and Entertainment Complex arrives at the dawning of New York's newfound relationship to its waterfront. In the last few years alone, ferry service has been reinstated between points in Manhattan and New Jersey, and extensive plans are underway to link Manhattan with points up the Hudson River and on Long Island. Unlike the static, "historic," restoration of the South Street Seaport, which created a "reminder" of what New York's waterfront was like, the Chelsea Piers Renovation creates a vital new center of urban activity along the waterfront.

The Butler Rogers Baskett Project invites utilization of the piers and the Hudson River waterfront as it attempts to unite the facilities with the urban network of the city by projecting the future use of the waterfront.

The Chelsea Piers Sports and Entertainment Complex occupies four reclaimed Piers, numbers 59 through 62, and a five block-long structure referred to as the Headhouse, which grounds the piers to the western shoreline along the Hudson River from 17th to 23rd Streets. These four piers along with the Headhouse were once part of the original set of nine piers that were designed at the early part of the 20th century to accommodate a new generation of transatlantic ocean liners.

For the original project, land was removed from Manhattan to accommodate the then new large ships like the Mauritania and Lusitania, which required 800 foot-long berths. The original structures, completed in 1912, were designed by the architects Warren and Wetmore, who were also responsible for the design of New York City's Grand Central Station.

The overall complex, as it stands today, is composed of Piers 59, 60, 61, and 62, which are parallel to each other and perpendicular to the Headhouse that is situated along the shoreline.

The eastern facade of the Headhouse faces the rest of the city and distinguishes the architecture of the piers from that of the regular grid of Manhattan. None of the original, monumental cast-concrete arches by Warren and Wetmore have remained on the east-facing facade of the building.

The details were inexplicably removed in 1963 when the piers were renovated for use as a cargo terminal and replaced by a low-maintenance, banal metal wall.

The Butler Rogers Baskett architects had to work with the dreariness of the metal facade that could not be replaced. Instead, the industrial surface was decorated with murals by artist John Clem Clarke and can be seen from blocks away. The facade also hosts a series of signs and graphics indicating the different venues at the different piers.

Prior to beginning the design process, Butler Rogers Baskett approached the State Historic Preservation Office to determine whether there was any historical designation for the piers.

They discovered that although they had not yet been officially designated, the long-span steel structures on Piers 60 and 61 had been recommended for placement on the National Registry of Historic Places.

Notwithstanding the tentative status of the designation, the architects were required to proceed in accordance with the guidelines defined for a landmark structure.

As the historic use of the piers for transatlantic shipping was no longer appropriate, the State Historic Preservation Office approved the use of the piers as a Sports and Entertainment Complex, but required that the architects rehabilitate the historically significant fabric of the piers.

When the developers and Butler Rogers Baskett arrived on the project, two of the four piers, 60 and 61, were covered with breathtaking expanses of unbroken interior space; and the remaining two piers, 59 and 62, were simply vast open platforms sitting above the water. Here the main slab is about five feet above mean high tide.

This situation required some of the work, including pile modification, new elevator pits, electrical conduit work, and underground plumbing to be performed from boats or by marine contractors and engineers, and forcing the contractor, A J Contracting to schedule construction around tide conditions.

Since the piers originally accommodated freight loading and gangways for passenger boarding, the exterior facades of the covered piers included large, overhead swinging doors at the second floor level some 25 feet above the ground.

Butler Rogers Baskett designed a new glazing pattern across the facade to reflect the original rhythm of the bay doors. Here the architects incorporated a four foot by four foot window in alternating bays together with an articulated mullion pattern that referred to the original fenestration pattern of the structure.

The architects designed new exterior stairs for five safety systems and located these covered structures along the facades of Piers 60 and 61 where gangways might once have been placed. These structures are an interesting illustration of how the architects resolved the problems that the oddity of the spaces presented, while simultaneously calling to mind a notion of the past life of the structures without falling into historical quotation.

The necessary stair structures provide emergency exits from the second-floor facilities on Piers 60 and 61, and were simply treated as awnings and covered in bright red fabric. In a quite contemporary way, this intervention obliquely refers to the movement of passengers from the upper decks of the no longer present transatlantic ocean liners.

The roofs on Piers 60 and 61 were replaced, and the entire steel structure of the piers was cleaned and painted.

The underwater structures were also rehabilitated as were the open spaces of Piers 59 and 62. The huge project is not only an example of how existing, outdated structures can be recycled and reincarnated,

The Butler Rogers Baskett architects had to work with the dreariness of the metal facade that could not be replaced. Instead the surface was decorated with murals by artist John Clem Clarke which can be seen from blocks away. Here a photo-montage shows a proposed facade treatment.

but it also represents one of the most ambitious private investments on the waterfront in any city in the United States.

The complex can be entered from the north at 23rd Street, onto an open plaza in front of Pier 62.

The architects created Sunset Strip, a north-south walkway through the project that runs parallel to the shoreline at the western edge of the Headhouse and offers views of the river, piers, and the interior public areas of the Headhouse.

The Butler Rogers Baskett team redirected automobile traffic around to the east facade and utilized the existing ground-floor entrances into the Headhouse and piers beyond. The ground level of Piers 60 and 61 were designated as parking areas and elevators connect these areas to the sports facilities above.

Chelsea Piers is impressive both for its enormous size and for the range of facilities it holds.

The $100 million project hosts between 8,000 and 10,000 visitors each day, including some 1,200 to 1,500 full- and part-time employees. The Field House alone is the setting for as many as 40 children's birthday parties every weekend.

The piers themselves, albeit in a limited way, continue to function.

There is a marina, a sailing school, and Spirit Cruises, operating out of Pier 61, which offers New York harbor dining.

Butler Rogers Baskett was faced with the challenge of fitting all the various venues and activities onto the piers and working within what was still, despite the 1960s desecration of its historic facade, an historic structure.

As the structures had already been partly demolished, the architects located the golf driving range on the open space of Pier 59, and placed the outdoor roller-skating rinks on Pier 62.

Piers 60 and 61, on the other hand, were intact, and the architects had to simultaneously create spaces that felt open and full of light, while retaining the original steel truss work. Pier 60 hosts the vast Sports Center health club with includes such oddities as a beach-volleyball court, a 55-foot climbing wall, the world's longest indoor running track, and the Origins Feel-Good Day Spa.

Pier 61 has become the new home to Sky Rink and hosts two of the cities most advanced ice-skating rinks.

The Butler Rogers Baskett architects and designers created a sports and entertainment center that clearly functions as an oasis of urban relief.

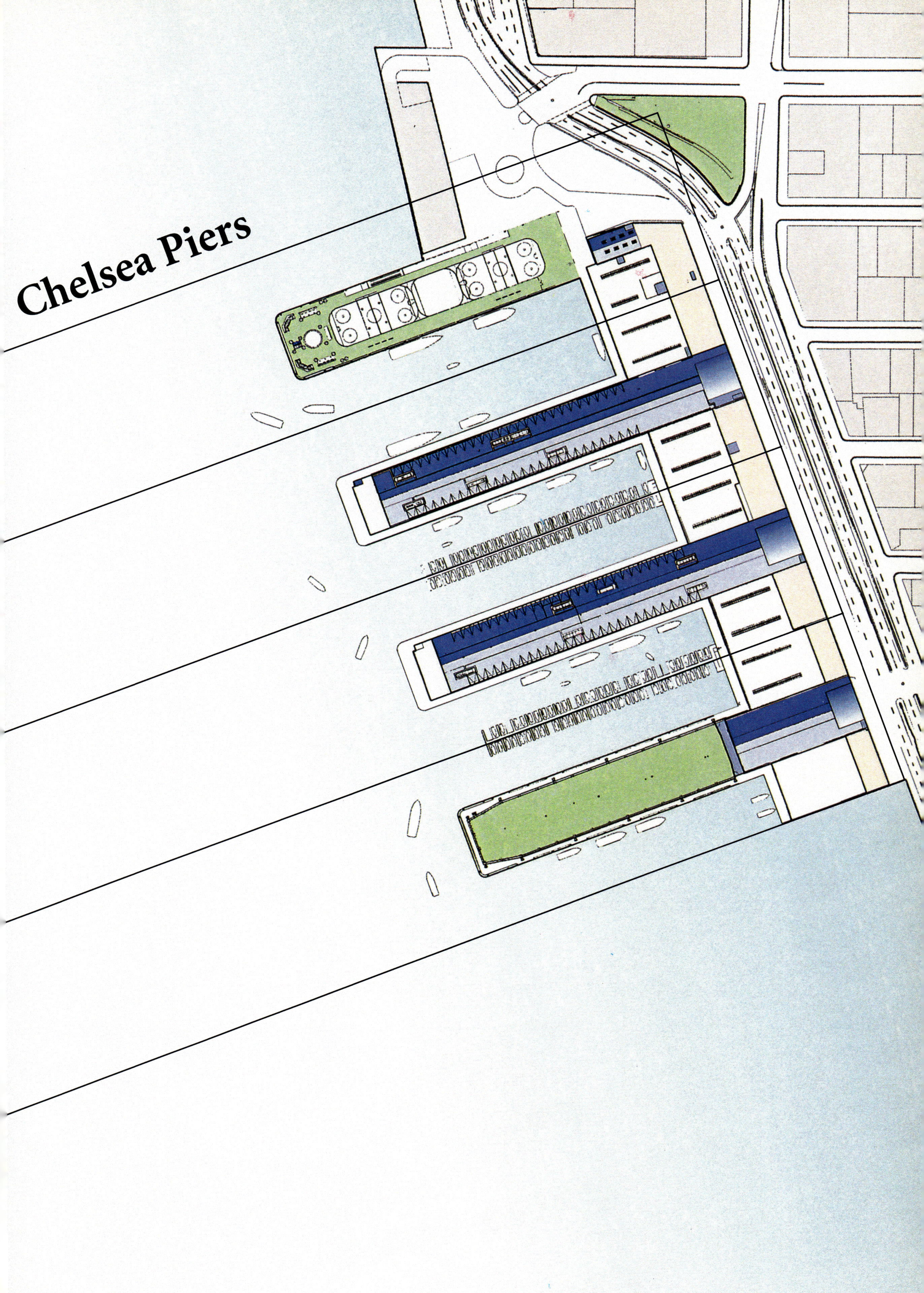

Chelsea Piers

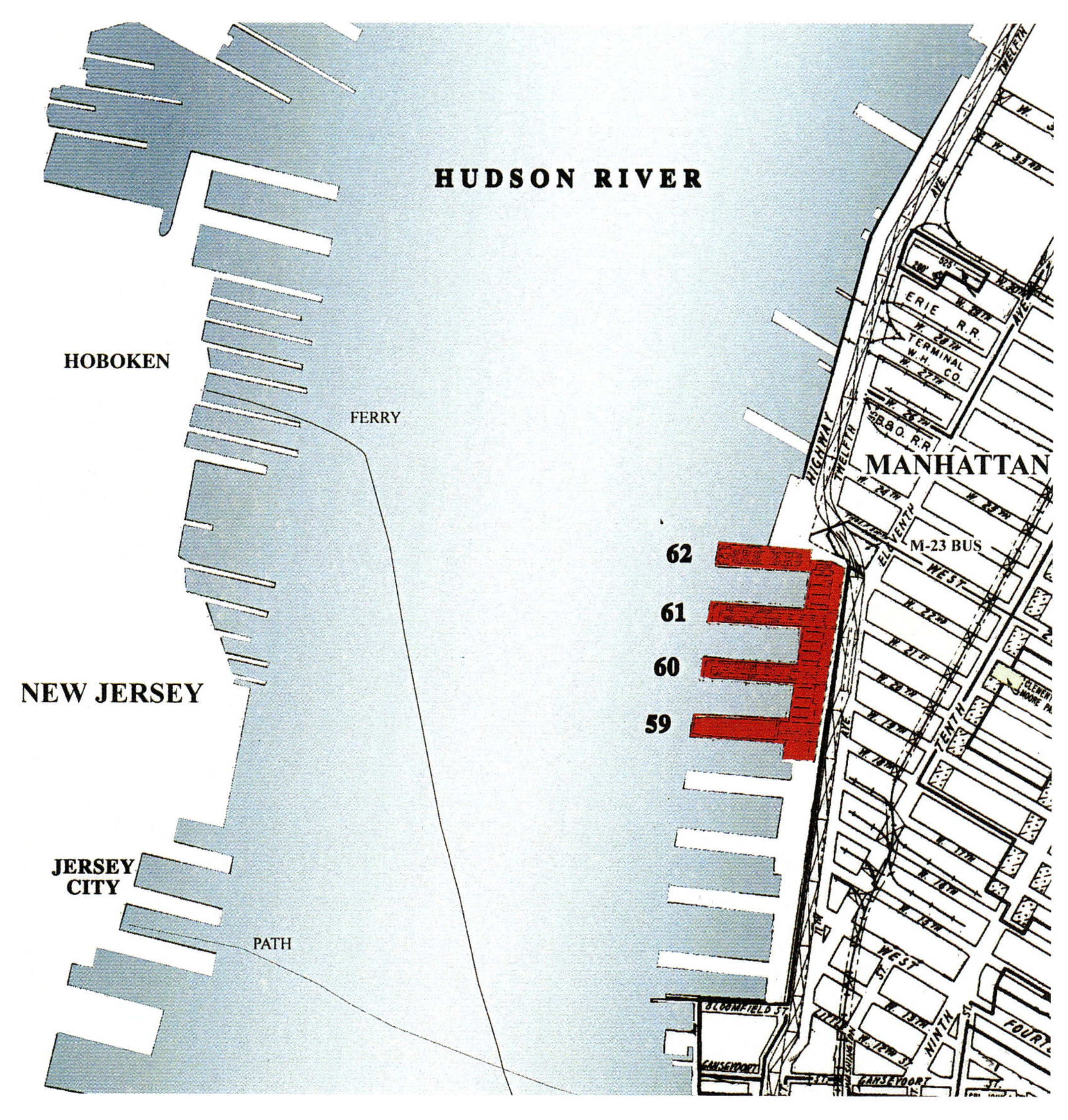

The Chelsea Piers Sports and Entertainment complex as it is situated on Manhattan's West Side, along the Hudson River from West 17th to West 23rd Streets. Below, longitudinal sections of Piers 59, 60, 61 and 62 illustrate the relationship the piers maintain to both the river and the land mass of Manhattan. The drawings also illustrate the maximization of space consistent with the various uses.

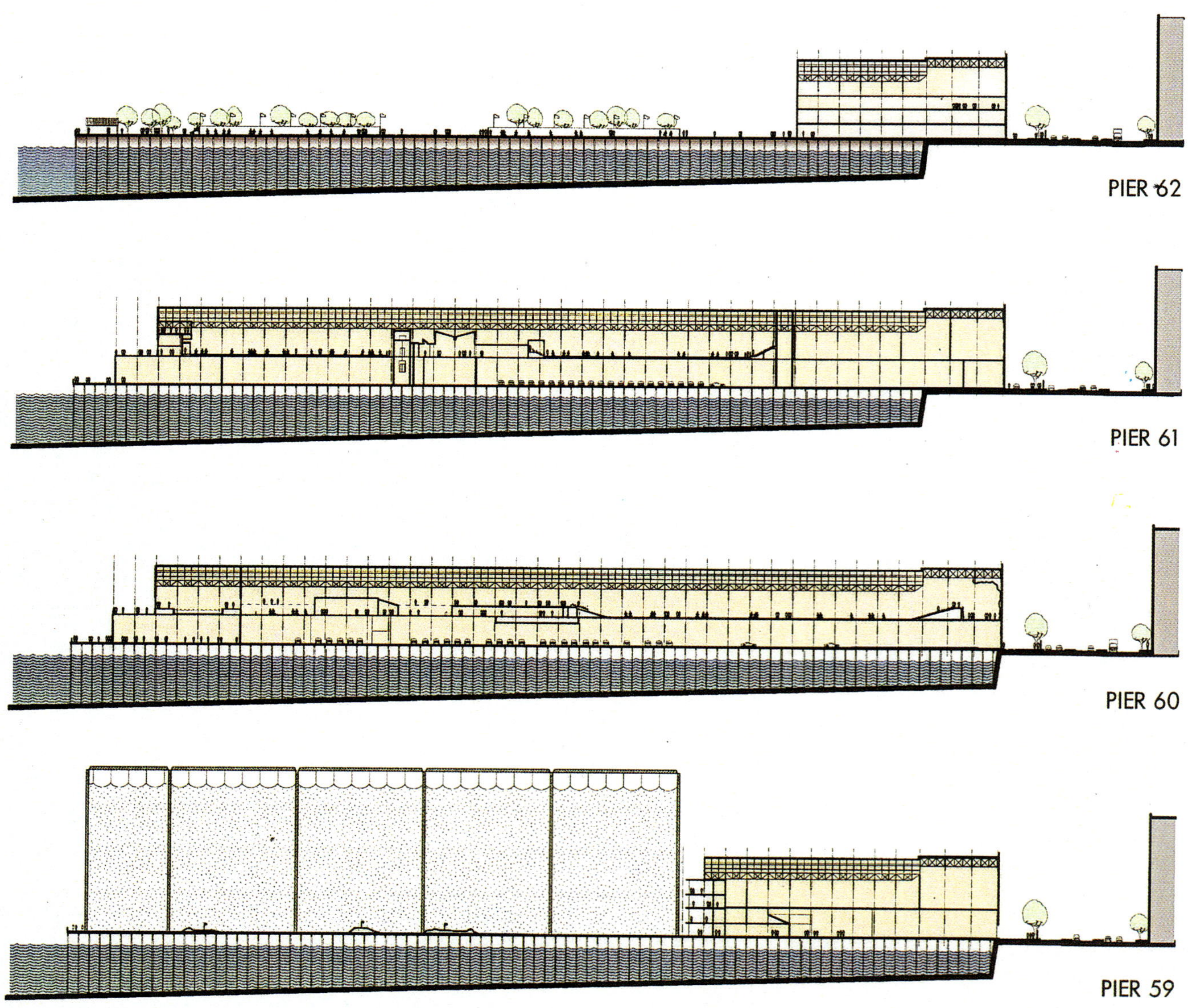

Left, ground floor plan as built showing the parking facilities within piers 60 and 61. At this level, elevator banks connect these areas to the sports facilities above. The drawing also illustrates the public access esplanade which winds along the perimeter of each of the piers.

Right, second floor plan as built illustrates the positioning of the two rinks within Pier 61 at Sky Rink and the running track within the Chelsea Piers Sports Center.

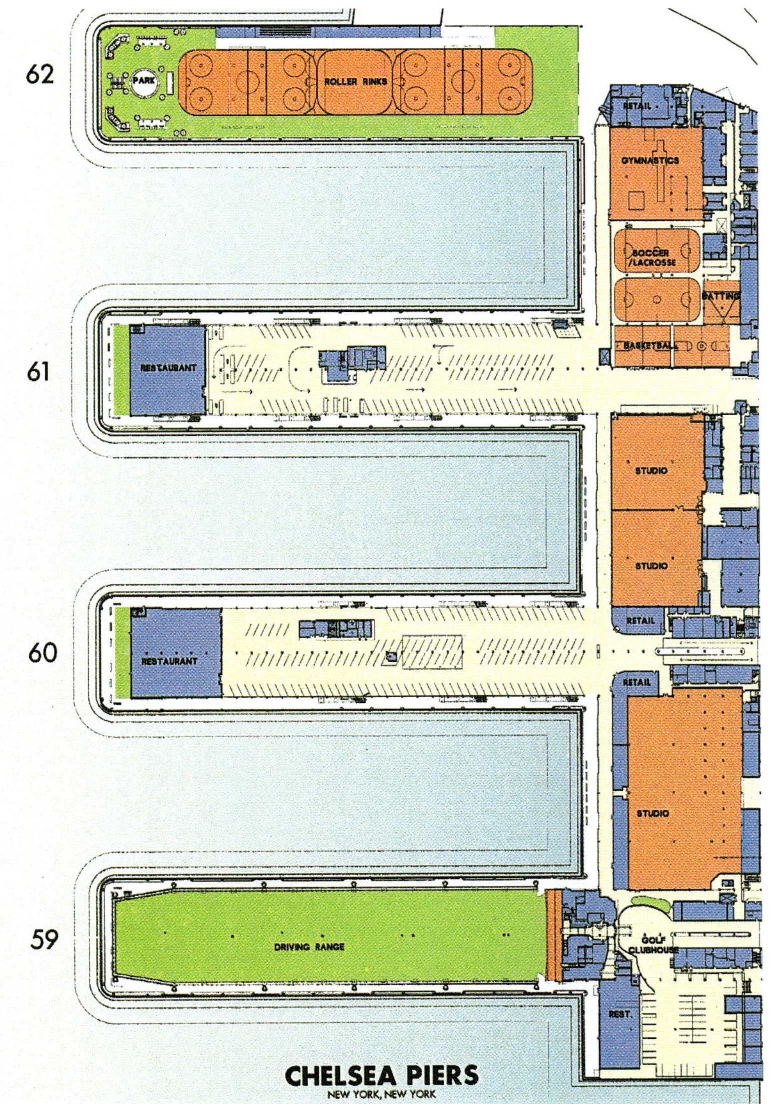

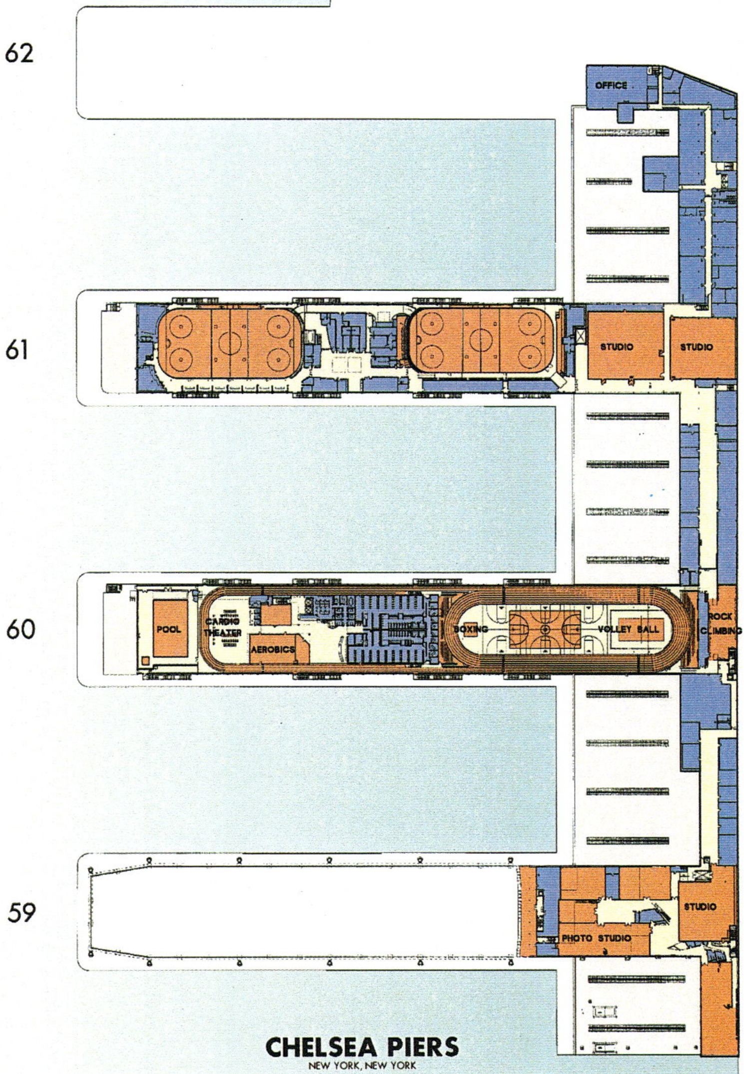

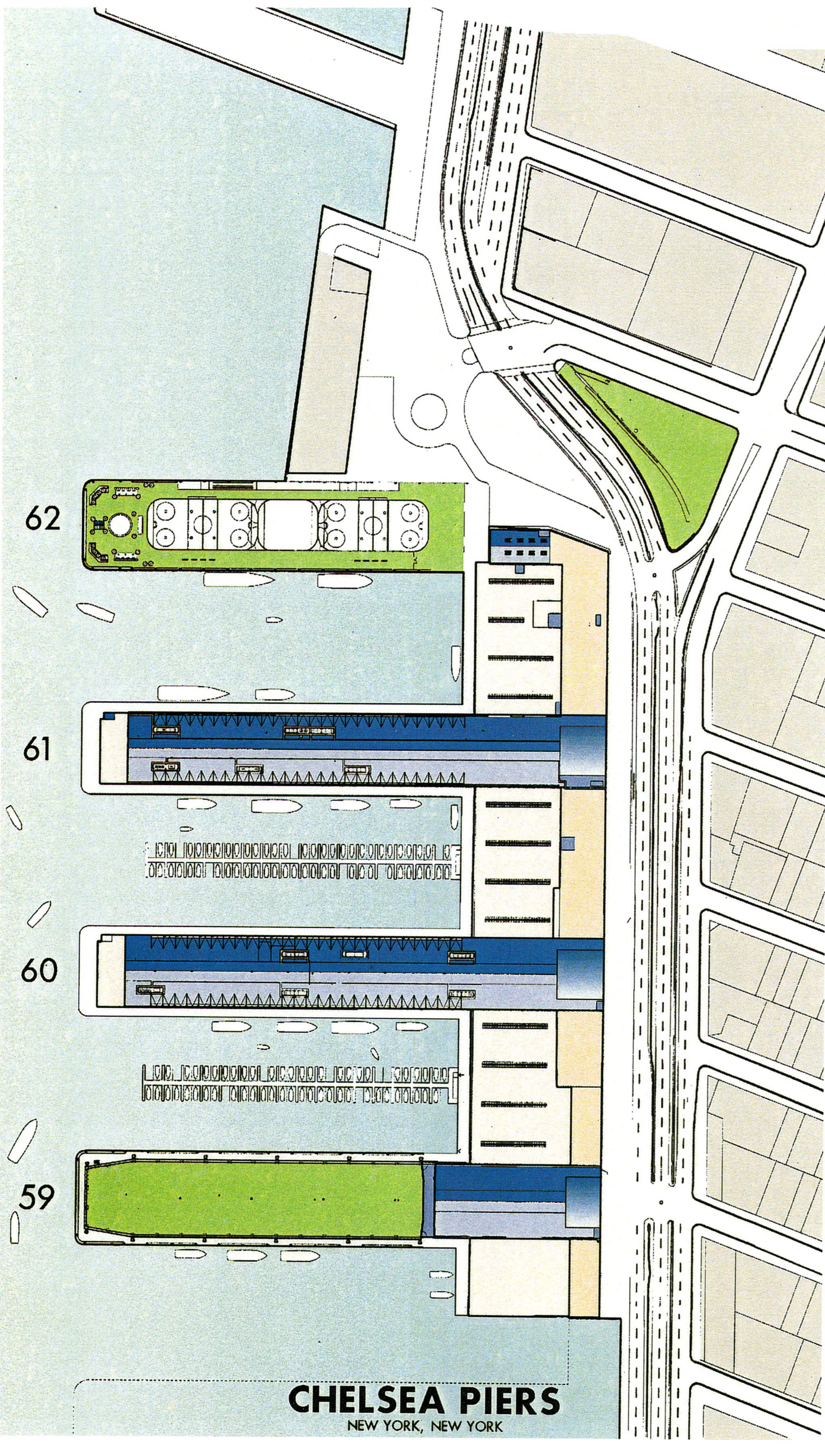

This site plan illustrates the magnitude of the Chelsea Piers Sports and Entertainment Complex as it spans north form West 17th Street to its entrance at West 23rd Street. The image also illustrates the potential vitality of the site as a major boating center.

Opposite page, this set of waterfront, street, and pier elevations express the various facade details. The program for this street elevation was inspired by the original facade and became an important part of the design in order to obtain landmarks approval. The pier elevations, as seen from across the Hudson River, express the window and facade details found on Piers 60 and 61 as well as the open facade and netting structures found on pier 59 at the Chelsea Piers Golf Club. The side elevation of one of the two covered piers shows the exit/egress stairs which are reminiscent of the gangways once used by passengers of the large transatlantic ships.

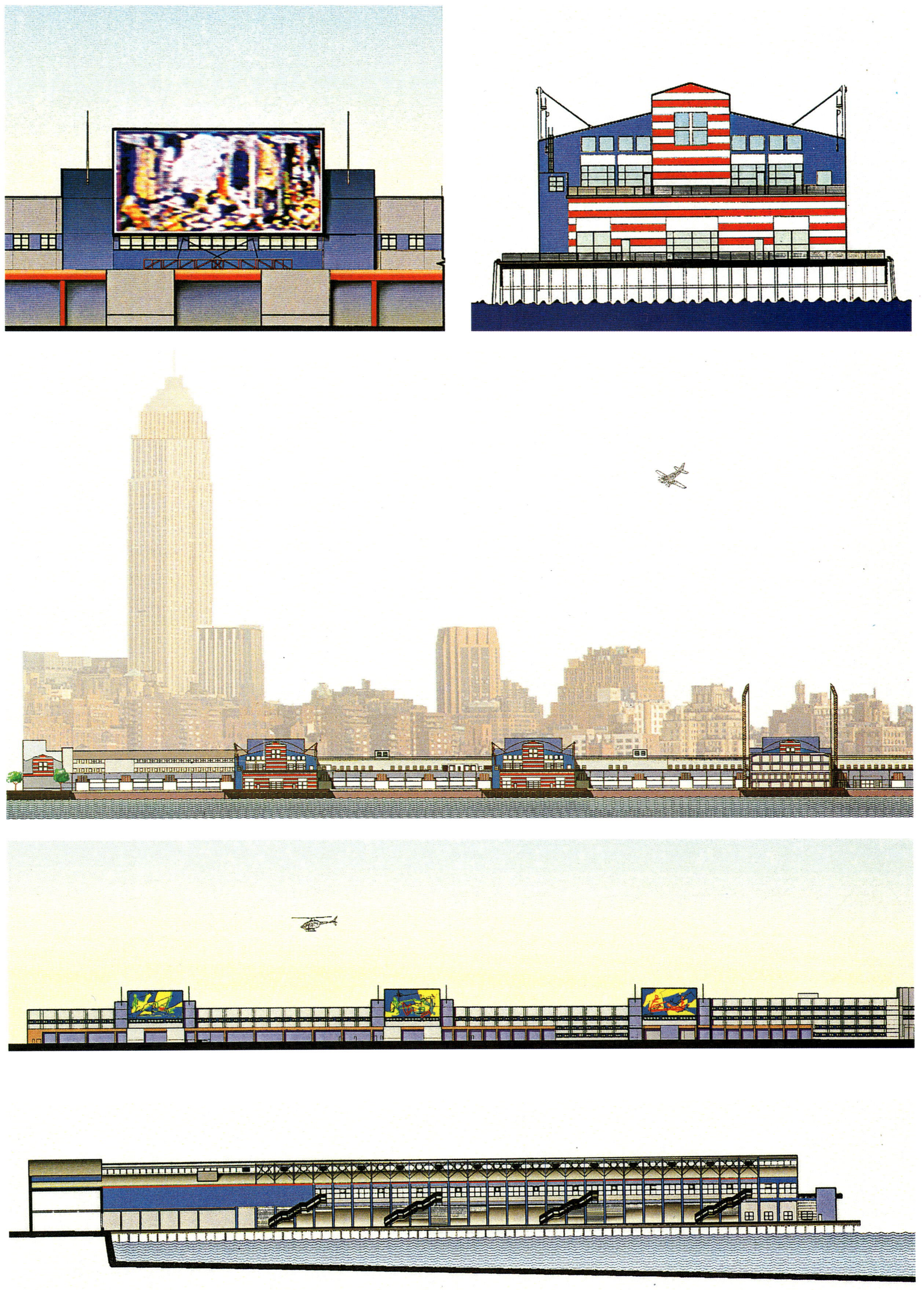

Headhouse

The Headhouse is a five-block-long structure which grounds the four piers to the western shoreline of Manhattan from 17th to 23rd Streets.

The vast structure hosts the Chelsea Piers Field House, Silver Screen Studios, and the largest fashion-photography facility in Manhattan. Silver Screen Studios is Manhattan's largest center for film and television production.

It is currently home to both ABC and NBC television productions as well as a studio for feature films. The newly renovated television and film studio is being referred to as "Hollywood-on-the-Hudson." The 250,000 square-foot space includes sound stages, production offices, studio-support space, carpentry and scenic painting shops, dressing rooms, and set storage. Parking and truck access is also available through the eastern facade.

The 30,000 square-foot fashion-photography studio is located on the second level.

The architects created an interior, weather-protected, north-south walkway, referred to as Sunset Strip, which extends behind the sound stages along the western edge of the Headhouse.

Sunset Strip connects the various athletic facilities as well as the 1.2 mile-long public esplanade as it winds along the river. In addition to windows into the Field House and various retail stores, the architects have installed large black and white photographs documenting the history of the Chelsea Piers along the interior wall to provide the passageway with a lively streetlike atmosphere. The Chelsea Maritime Center also adds vitality to the scene as a variety of luxury yachts, dinner boats, sail and power boats, deep-sea fishing boats, and kayaks can be observed.

The Chelsea Piers Maritime Center is destined to become Manhattan's largest and most diverse marina.

Construction plan of Chelsea Piers management offices.

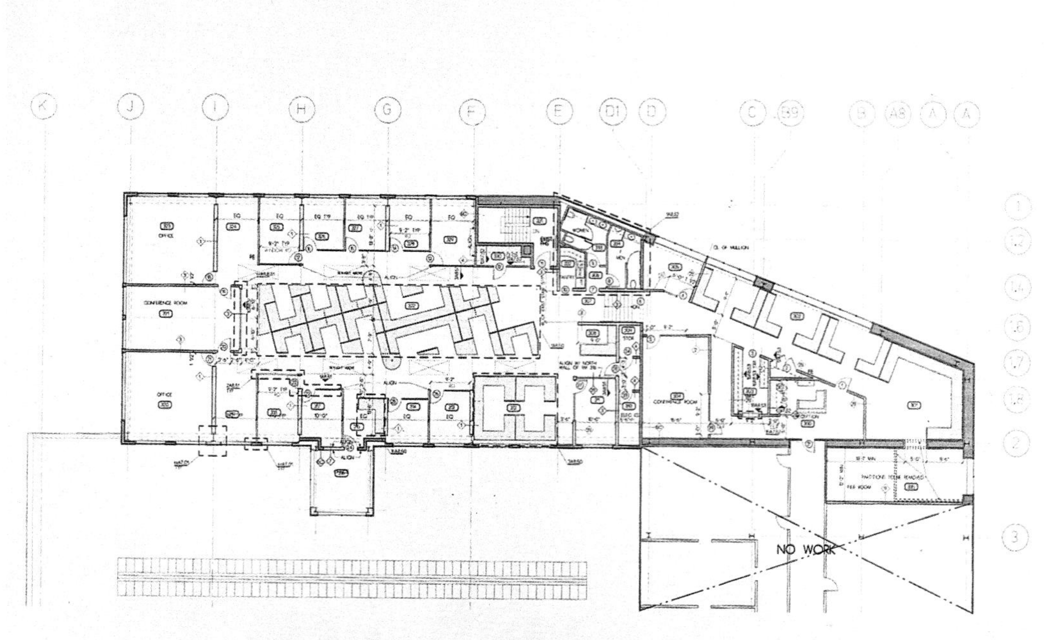

Below, the Headhouse at the Chelsea Piers Sports and Entertainment Complex as it exists today with automobile and pedestrian entries to Piers 61, 60, and 59.

Right, historical photograph from New York City's Bettman Archive illustrates the Headhouse as it was originally constructed.

The Chelsea Piers
Headhouse as viewed
form the West Side
Highway. Here the entry
to Sky Rink is
prominently indicated
with bold graphics and
one of the three John
Clem Clarke murals.

PIER 61
CHELSEA PIERS
SPORTS & ENTERTAINMENT
THE CRAB HOUSE
SKY RINK
SPIRIT CRUISES
SKY RINK
CHELSEA PIERS

Above, view into
conference room
at the Chelsea Piers
management offices
located within
the Headhouse.
Below, typical corridor
at the Chelsea Piers
management offices
located within the
Headhouse.

Chelsea Piers Headhouse
and taxi/bus drop off
area with cars at guard
house.
Below, Chelsea Piers
Headhouse with views
to the south and west.

CHELSEA PIERS
SPORTS & ENTERTAINMENT
ROLLER RINKS
CHELSEA PIERS

Right, the interior, north-south walkway which connects the various athletic facilities within the Headhouse referred to as Sunset Strip. Here visitors are provided with a view into the Gymnastics Center. Below, the Chelsea Piers Sports and Entertainment Complex waterfront esplanade as it connects Pier 61 and 60. The 1.2 mile-long public space offers wonderful views of the Hudson River as it winds along the perimeter of each of the piers.

In addition to windows into the Headhouse and various retail stores, large black and white photographs documenting the history of the Chelsea Piers were installed along the interior wall of Sunset Strip.

On the following pages, looking south from West 23rd Street, the Chelsea Piers Sports and Entertainment Complex clearly communicates a spirit of vitality, movement, and leisure. Here the Spirit Cruse Boats are in view as they are docked at Pier 61, and in the distance one can see the netting structures rising above the Chelsea Piers Golf Club driving range on Pier 59.

CHELSEA PIERS
SPORTS & ENTERTAINMENT
Manhattan
Mini Storage

Field House

The Chelsea Piers Field House is located at the northernmost part of the Headhouse structure, between Piers 62 and 61. The 80,000-square-foot facility represents Manhattan's premier facility for gymnastics, team sports, and league playing.

The facilities include New York State's largest competitive gymnastics center, and the only facility in New York City sanctioned by the USGA, United States Gymnastics Association, for state, regional, and national competitions.

There are also two hardwood basketball courts, two artificial turf playing fields for indoor soccer and lacrosse, spectator seating for 500, four batting cages, dance studios, a martial arts mezzanine, a climbing wall designed especially for children, and a child-care center.

The 23,000-square-foot gymnastics facility is equipped with competition spring floors, deep-foam training pits, sunken trampolines, and in-ground tumble tracks.

The facility hosts Olympic-quality equipment for both men's and women's events, including balance beam, isometric bars, high bar, parallel bars, still rings, pommel horse and vaults. The facility also hosts a toddler's gym where children up to age four can learn to tumble and develop athletic skills.

Throughout the Field House the architects created a sense of dynamic energy that seems to empower both children and adults alike. Here the architects used bright colors, not only in the vast array of colored mats and foam-filled pits, but in every detail of the architecture as well. Shades of green are used together with reds and pinks; it is all yellow and orange, sun-light and action. The simple architectural theme of a ppitched roof house is repeated with both striped awnings over interior structures and highly colored silhouettes of structures along the perimeter of the space.

All of this activity opens onto Sunset Strip and the river beyond with large windows that create a theatrical event of the display of energy within.

Opposite page, proposed elevations of the Field House showing color palette inspired by the Caribbean Islands. Here different colors were used to define and indicate different activities and uses.

Below, like all the facilities within the Field House, this batting cage hosts state-of-the-art equipment in an atmosphere that radiates with energy and light.

Below, the Program Registration Desk and adjoining corridor also reflect the Caribbean inspired palette which runs throughout the Field House.

Right, the Gymnastics facility within the Field House features a gymnastics training pit. The architects had to cut into the pier slab to house the pits and its foam blocks are actually sitting below the high tide water level.

The original structural
steel work within the
Field House was painted
with bright colors
to become part
of the overall design.
Here the blue and red
of the basketball courts
is continued into
the treatment of the
structure above.

Field House, basketball
courts.

In these pages, Chelsea
Piers Field House
lacrosse/soccer/ field
hockey playing field.

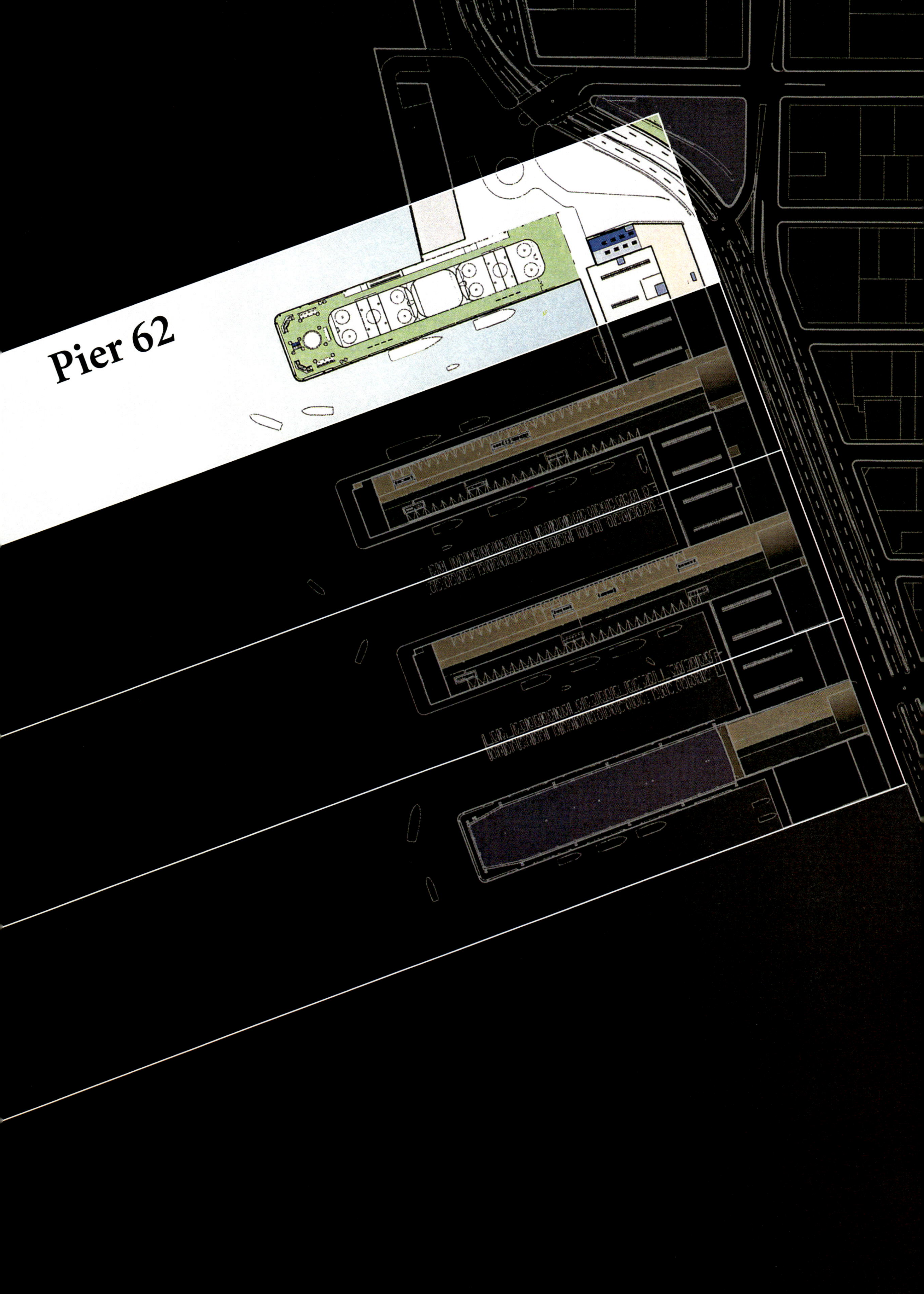
Pier 62

Roller Rinks and Pier Park

Pier 62, like Pier 59, was an uncovered slab of concrete lying just above the surface of the water and extending some 880 feet into the Hudson River.

The Butler Rogers Baskett architects decided to transform this barren plateau at the northernmost edge of the complex into a two-and-one-half acre open air Pier Park. With the help ot Landscape architect Edmund Hollander. Because of its location near the 23rd Street entrance to the entire Chelsea Piers Sports and Entertainment Complex, the architects conceived of the Pier Park as both a threshold to the various public and private venues, and as a public center for both outdoor recreation and waterside relaxation. The architects flanked the entrance here with two fragments of the original Warren and Wetmore structure to welcome visitors to the complex and to create a reminder of the pier's past.

At the pier's western edge the architects placed a landscaped public park with benches and picnic tables where visitors can enjoy the river views that include the Statue of Liberty and the Verrazzano Narrows Bridge to the south, the Manhattan skyline to the east, and the New Jersey Palisades across the river to the west.

It is from this public park that the 20-foot-wide, 1.2-mile-long esplanade that runs along the perimeter of each of the piers starts. In addition to the outdoor public spaces, Pier 62 also hosts two outdoor, regulation-sized, professionally surfaced in-line roller-skating rinks.

The architects placed skate-rental facilities on the ground floor of the nearby Headhouse, and created an open square of activity as skaters approach the rinks from the skate-rental area or rest at the sidelines.

The rinks themselves, which can be united to form one 650-foot-long rink, are available for league play or general skating.

This illustration shows the proposed plans for the public park on Pier 62. Opposite page, the northern end of the Headhouse at the entrance to Pier 62 is here in view. A new retail store along with skate rental shop were located within the Headhouse and a directory to the Chelsea Piers Sports and Entertainment Complex boldly appears on the pavement.

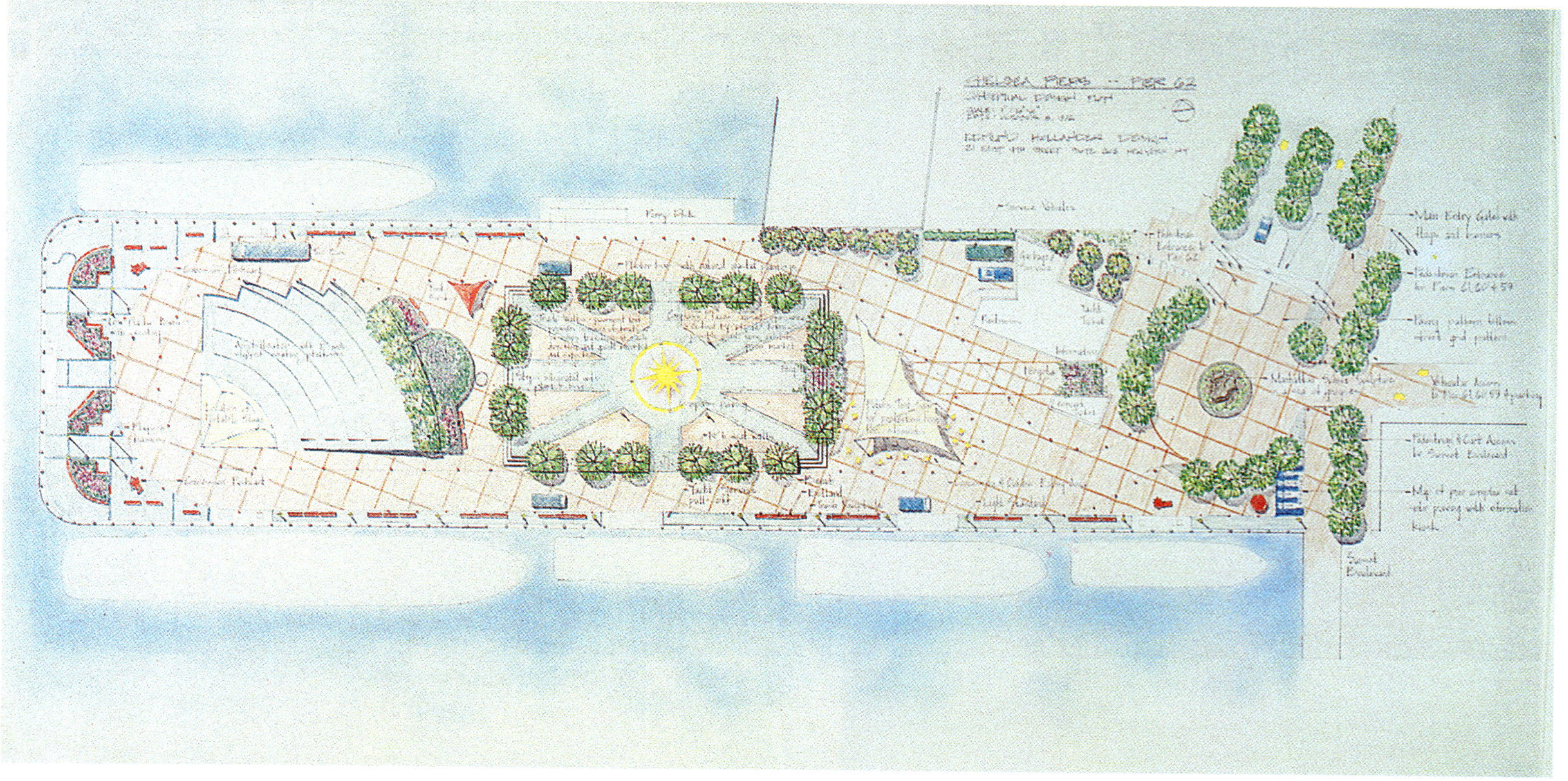

BLADES
Board & Skate
ROLLER RINKS
CHELSEA PIERS
TICKETS
THE CHELSEA PIERS
COMPANY STORE
MAIN ENTRANCE
FIELD HOUSE
SKY RINK
ROLLER

The Roller Rinks and the
entire length of Pier 62
are here in view from
the pier's western end.

CHELSEA PIERS

An historical element, Griffin Wing, was taken from original structures along the West Side Highway and incorporated into the grounds of Pier 62 to mark an important entrance.

A view of the Pier Park sign with the Chelsea Piers Headhouse in the background.

Opposite page, detail of the Headhouse which illustrates how an addition was made to the west-facing facade. Here the metal facade was revitalized by the architects to become part of the total design program.

MAIN

The northern end
of the Headhouse
is seen here as well as
the automobile and bus
drop-off area/entrance to
the Chelsea Piers Sports
and Entertainment
Complex at the northern
end of the Pier Park.

Walkways around the Chelsea Piers Roller Rinks are shown here with the Empire State Building rising above in the background.

A view of the southern
side of the Pier Park with
the Roller Rink to left
and Headhouse
in background.

A sunset view of the
Roller Rinks at Pier 62
as seen from the public
area at Sunset Strip.

A view of the Pier Park with the Roller Rinks in the background.

Pier 61

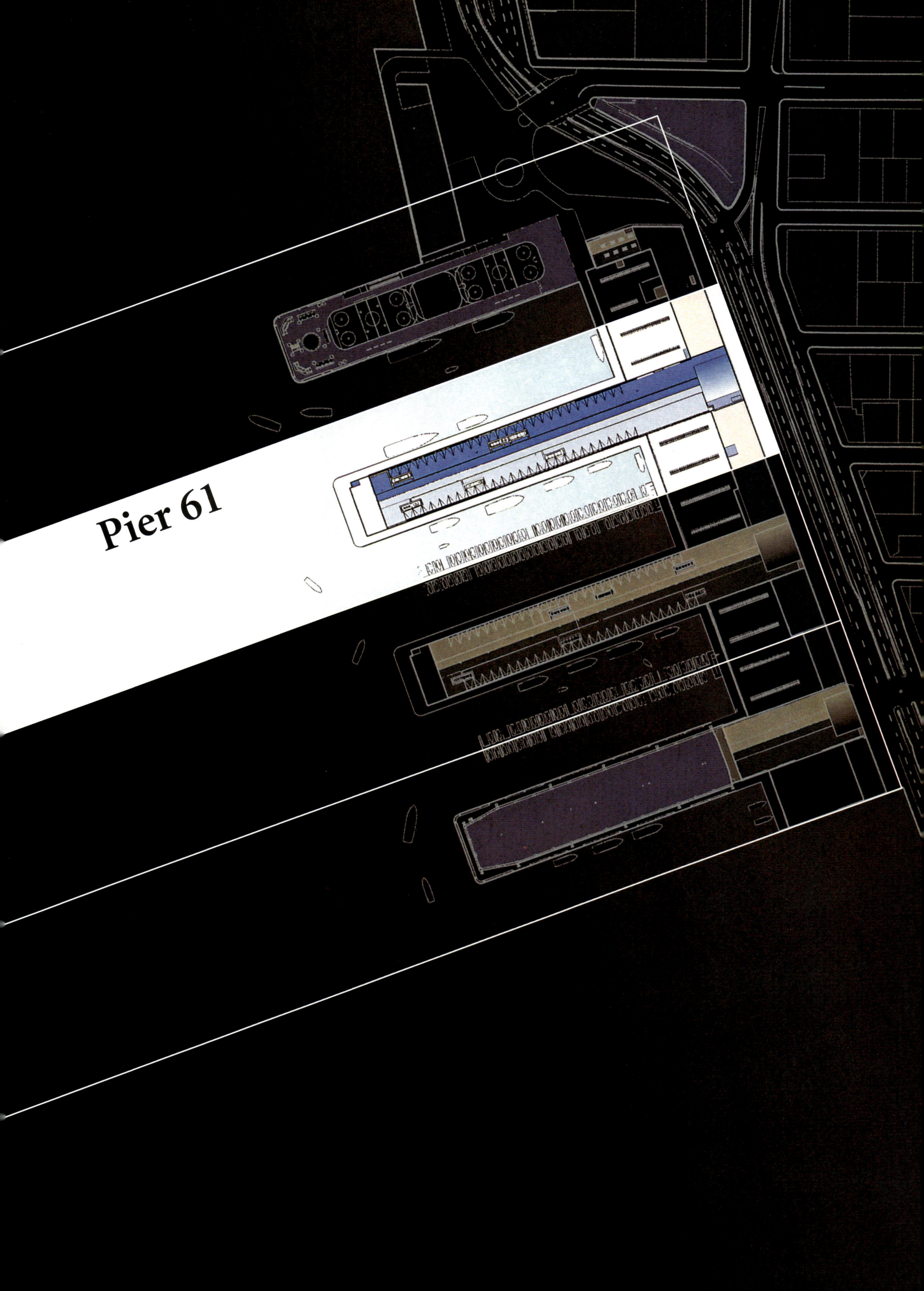

Sky Rink

Sky Rink is located on Pier 61, one of the two covered structures that the architects had to work with. Like the Sports Center on Pier 60, Sky Rink can be reached by crossing a ground-level parking facility to arrive at the center of the pier.

From this point elevators carry visitors to the ice-skating facilities on the second floor.

Here the architects created a central space that serves as a reception area and an informal lounge with skate-rental facilities, concession stand, restrooms, and the East and West Rinks located at either end.

The architects painted this space with dramatic horizontal red and white stripes that call to mind the colors used in hockey uniforms.

Both of the rinks here offer expansive views of the sky and water. While the Olympic-sized West Rink is available for casual skaters, the regulation-sized East Rink offers the opportunity to host serious competitions and performances as it also offers seating for 1,800 spectators.

Sky Rink at Pier 61 is one of the premier ice-skating facilities in the United States, and the only year-round ice-skating rink in Manhattan.

The two full-sized ice-skating rinks offer a varied and flexible schedule for both training and recreation, as well as programs and exhibitions for figure-skaters and hockey players.

Within the skating areas, the architects enhanced the cool feeling of the blue-white ice by painting the original truss work a deep green color and using a bright blue on the floors and railings.

In addition to the areas open to the public, the architects also created two Sky Boxes suspended over the rinks and a private party room located at the west end of the pier.

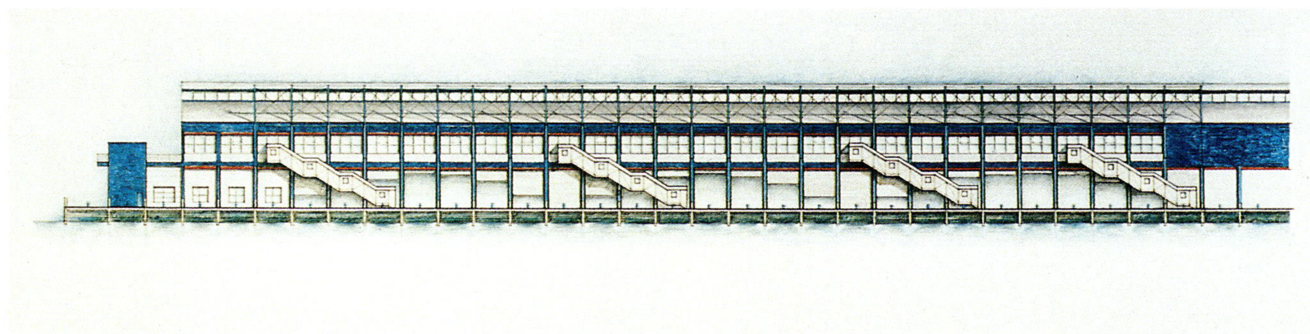

Rendering of the
southern facade
of Pier 61.
Below, Pier 61 as seen
from Pier 62.

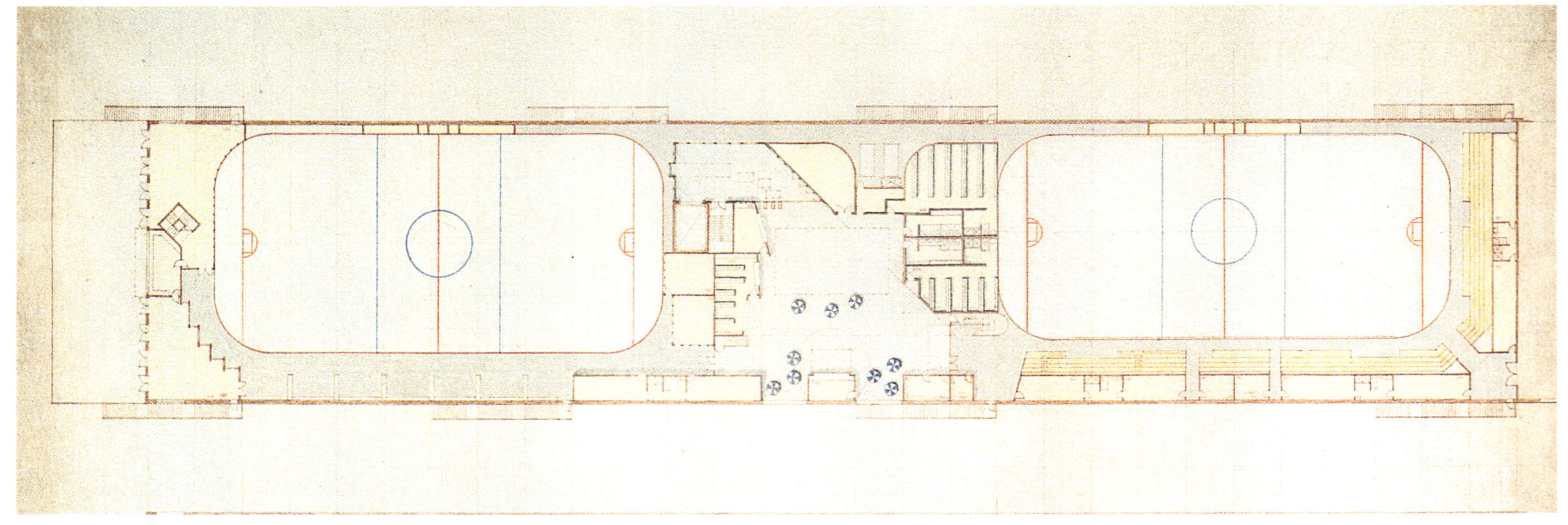

Top and right, plans
of Sky Rink during early
developmental stages.
Pier 61 as seen from
Pier 62.

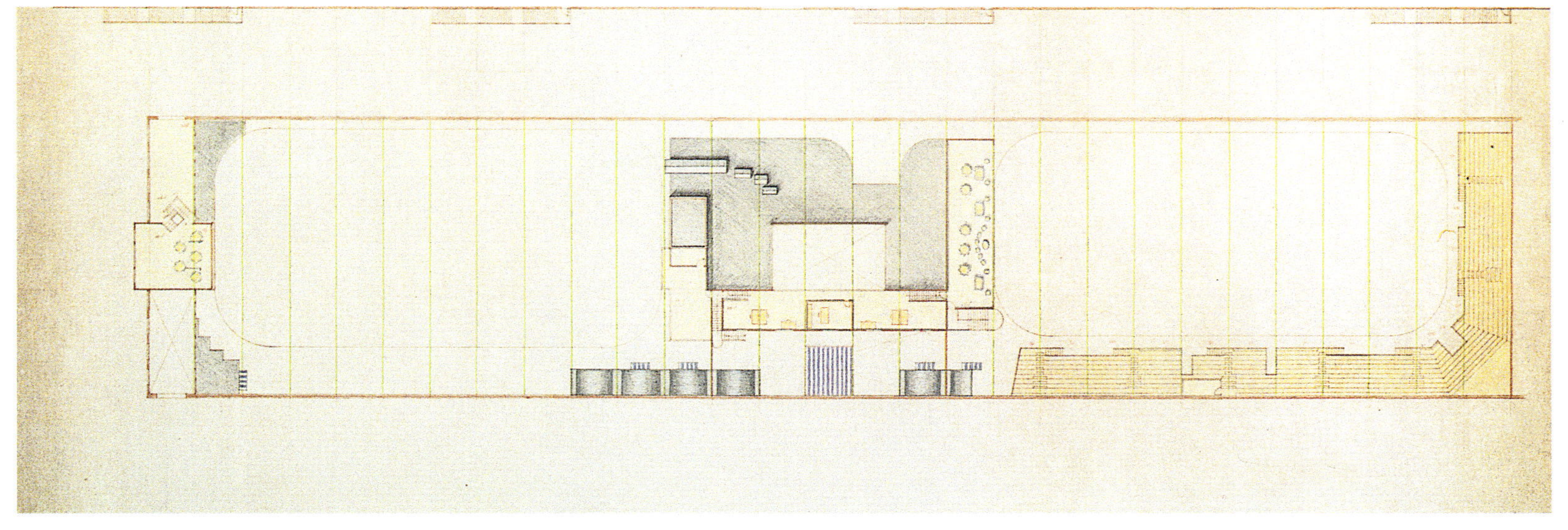

The exterior of Pier 61
as seen from the outdoor
public space showing the
stairs before they were
covered.

This image of Pier 61
shows how the
restaurant facility was
placed at the end of the
lower level and how
Sky Rink was developed
above. The image also
illustrates how the
outdoor public space
wraps around the
perimeter of the pier.

Sky Rink, a sun filled
view of corridor on
south side of West Rink
with the entrance
to the "Olympic Village"
beyond the exit doors.

Sky Rink, these views
of south side corridor
show the flow of natural
light into the lofty blue
and green space.

Previous page, the
exterior of Pier 61 as
visitors board a waiting
boat.

The public esplanade winds
around Pier 61 to meet the
ground-level, open-air-
dining facility of a restaurant
located at western end of
Pier 61. The restaurant is a
private venue that was not
designed by Butler Rogers
Baskett.

This exterior view
of Pier 61 shows that
the overhead doors
at the ground level can
be opened onto the
parking area beneath
Sky Rink.

Opposite page, the
exterior of Pier 61 shows
the fire safety exits for
Sky Rink which were
designed to call to mind
the passenger gangways
of the transatlantic ships
that once docked here.

Above, Sky Rink, in addition to the areas open to the public, the architects also created two Sky Boxes suspended over the rinks at the west end of the pier.

Below, the red and white horizontal striped space between the East Rink and the West Rink is known as the "Olympic Village". Here locker rooms, skate rental, pro-shop, and snack bar are located.

Sky Rink, West Rink,
here bright colors were
used on the original
steel structure and
for the bold graphics
in the background. With
windows on both the
northern and southern
sides of the pier, the
entire rink has an open,
light-filled feeling.

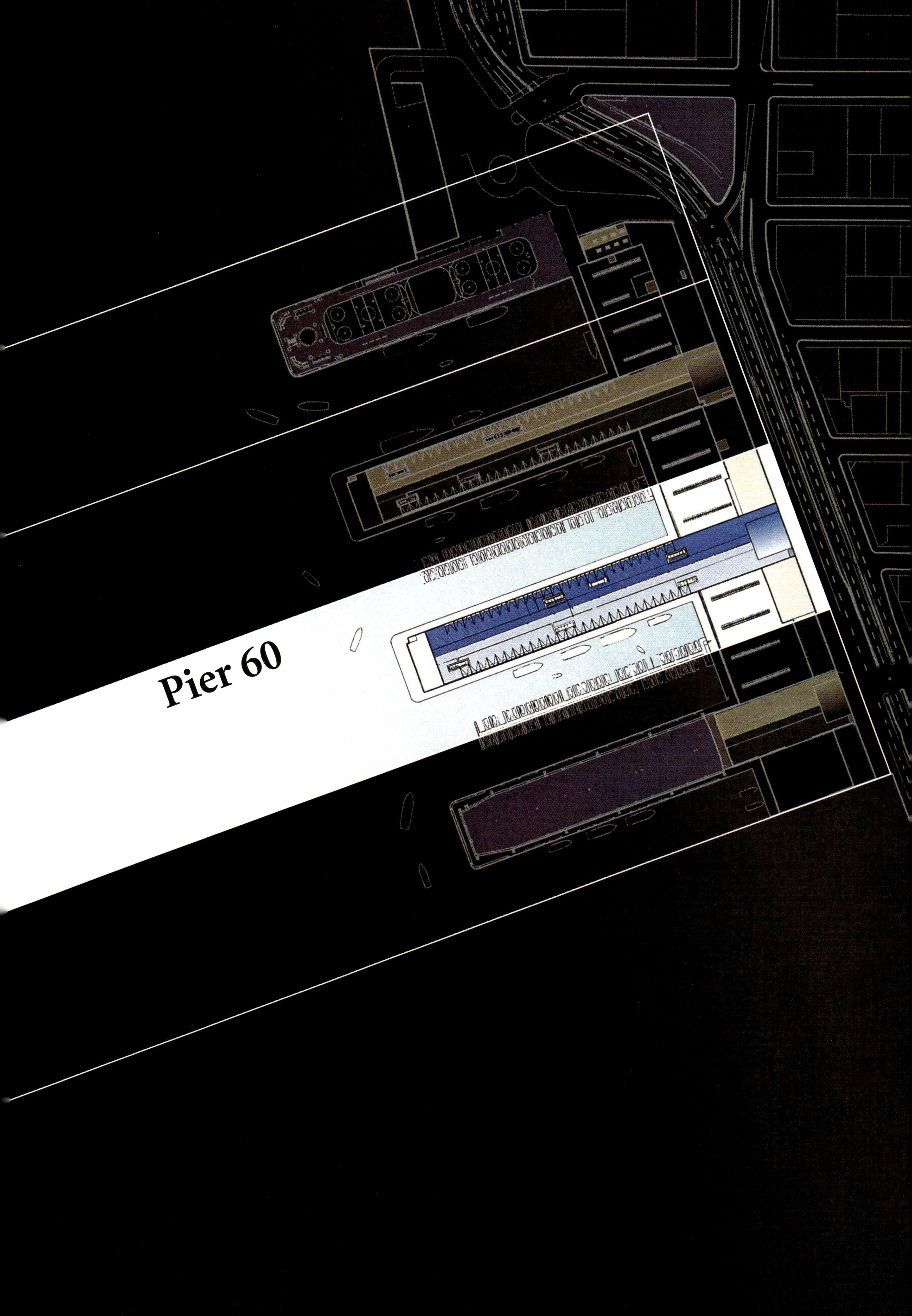

Pier 60

Sports Center

Pier 60 hosts the 150,000 square-foot Sports Center. Three football fields long, enclosed on three sides by windows that offer views of the Statue of Liberty and the World Trade Center; it takes several minutes to walk from one end of this state-of-the-art facility to the other. In addition to providing space for endless quantities and variations of equipment, the Butler Rogers Baskett team created a multilevel sports facility that is everything that most Manhattan gyms are not: it is an exuberant, light-filled space that, despite the endless skyline views and early-20th-century ironwork overhead, provides its members with a bizarre, almost surreal relationship to nature.

The architects took full advantage of the position literally above the glittering river that surrounds three sides of the peninsula-like structure, to create a sports facility that immediately initiates a notion of action and movement, while simultaneously creating an effect that is distanced from the rest of New York in its ability to soothe and relax.

Unlike the other venues at the Chelsea Piers, the vast Sports Center is a membership facility. Here the Butler Rogers Baskett team created a space that is more private and luxurious than the other venues at Chelsea Piers, but simultaneously energy charged. The membership facility includes a burgundy-colored, 1/4 mile indoor jogging track, which is said to be the longest in the world; a 200 meter banked competition track; a track infield that can accommodate field events; basketball and volleyball courts; an indoor sand volleyball court; an extensive selection of cardiovascular and weight-training equipment; aerobic studios; boxing; spa facilities; a water-side sundeck; an indoor swimming pool; a fiberglass and pulverized granite rock climbing wall (the largest in the Northeastern United States); and a sports medicine center operated by a leading hospital. The facility also hosts arena seating for 1,750 spectators, men's and women's locker rooms, a juice and coffee bar, and, like Pier 61, covered parking at ground level.

Even the elaborate 90-year-old ironwork overhead has been sanitized in burgundy paint. The view south out the gigantic windows at the grimy, paint-flecked shell of Pier 57 (still an MTA bus-repair shop) comes off as irony— the surrounding cityscape as abstract as wallpaper.

The architects located the running track around the perimeter of the window-lined rectangular space and in doing so created a center island or core that was then developed on various levels. The entire design for the Sports Center seems to take its inspiration from the seductive pleasure of spectator sports. A suspended walkway brings swimmers from the locker rooms to the pool, but also provides excellent views into the aerobics rooms, the cardiovascular area, and the running track, for example. The architects used stadium seating to create both a ramp between the weight-training level and the ball courts, and while doing so invited members to sit and observe the activities within the boxing and the courts beyond. While sitting at the juice and coffee bar one can look out over the tables to a section of track that occasionally exposes a flash of runners and the lower Manhattan skyline beyond.

To enter the Sports Center, one must walk to the middle of the pier where an elevator core carries members to the facility on the second level. Upon entering the Sports Center there is a reception area and a coffee and food bar. A burgundy, gray, yellow, black, and beige carpet, designed by the Butler Rogers Baskett team, immediately informs visitors of the private character of the space and creates a perception of domestic as opposed to the institutional.

The carpet also functions as a means of introducing the colors and forms that are present within the entire area.

In the main space the architects created a clever event of the original truss structures and the new continuous band of the running track. Both the ironwork and the track are of the same rich burgundy color, and both, either seemingly or actually, tie the vast space together. While the high-tech track creates a sort of hovering, ribbon-like package around the

central core of the facility, the 90-year-old ironwork outlines the original structure and carries the monumental roof into the pier and river below. Overhead massive duct work, lighting, and video monitors not only weave through, hang from and are hooked onto the burgundy truss work, but also make the space feel like a very new and vital structure.

The architects have removed the central core area from the windows by the running track, and therefore have created the illusion of both indoor and outdoor space within the structure. The indoor pool was placed at the tip of the structure, and here again, one has the feeling of going out to the pool even if it is clearly within the structure.

The architects have manipulated the space of the Sports Center to fuse notions of indoor and outdoor, spectator and participant sports. The result is space that is simultaneously urban and distant from the city, relaxing and invigorating.

The Aerobics Room at
the Chelsea Piers Sports
Center was placed
within the central core
of the space, just off the
reception area.

The Cardio Deck at the
Chelsea Piers Sports
Center was built on
a raised floor to allow
for the flexibility of the
location and the type
of equipment. The use
of such flooring both
eliminates exposed
cables and avoids costly
electrical work as
the needs of the space
change.

View of worlds longest indoor running track at the Chelsea Piers Sports Center. Here the 1/4 mile-long track was installed along the perimeter of the structure and creates a belt within which the other facilities are located.

The swimming pool, located at the western end of the Chelsea Piers Sports Center on Pier 60, hosts the same color palette that is found in the locker rooms.

The juice bar at the Chelsea Piers Sports Center is located across from the reception area. The space features carpet that was designed by the architects. From this area visitors are provided with views of the running track on the same level and other activities above.

Opposite page, Chelsea Piers Sports Center, a view of a mezzanine level exercise area and the juice bar on the lower, entry level. Here the 90-year-old steel structure above has clearly become a design element.

View of waterside sun deck adjacent to pool in Chelsea Piers Sports Center on Pier 60. Below, view of whirlpool located at the southwest end of the Chelsea Piers Sports Center on Pier 60.

Opposite page, Chelsea Piers Sports Center sun deck situated beyond the swimming facility on the western end of Pier 60.

Two views of the locker
rooms at the Chelsea
Piers Sports Center. Here
the carpeting was
carried into the dressing
area and the tile work
at the pool side was
continued into the
shower and washing
area.

Chelsea Piers Sports
Center, an exercise area
sits comfortably beneath
the original steel
structure and is
illuminated from above
by side lights along
the roof line.

The exterior of Pier 60 as viewed from the public esplanade between Pier 61 and 60.

Opposite page, the western end of Pier 60 with the Chelsea Piers Sports Center sun deck located on the second level and the netting structure of the Chelsea Piers Golf Club's driving range on Pier 59 in the background.

Pier 60 as seen in the evening.

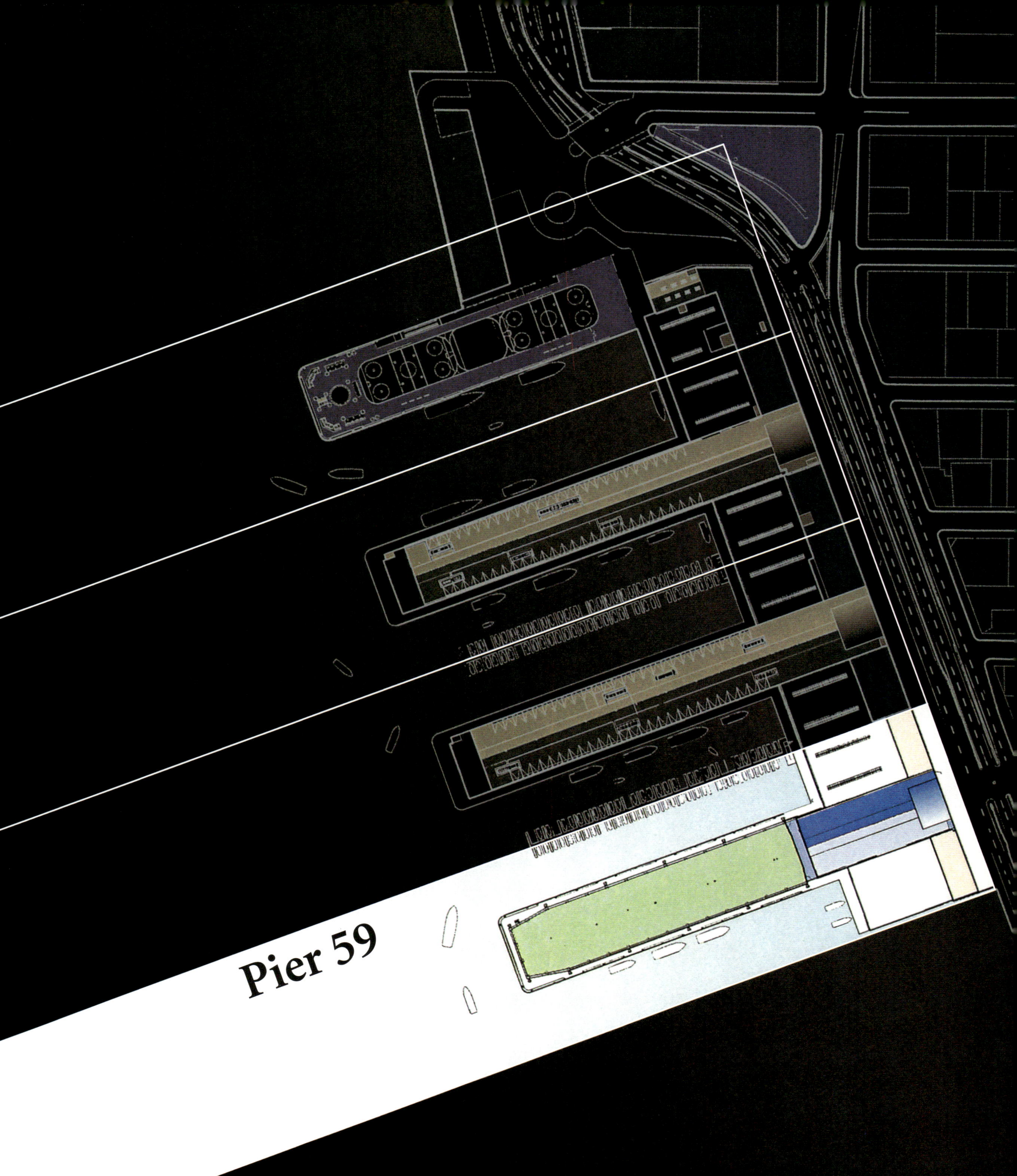

Pier 59

Golf Club

Like few other sports, golf calls to mind notions of open spaces. While resourceful New Yorkers have always found ways of incorporating basketball courts into parks, vacant lots, and parking areas, for example, golf remained a sport grounded in the wealth of open spaces, contact with manicured nature, and the suburban country club set.

When faced with the challenge of bringing golf to Manhattan the Butler Rogers Baskett decided to play into the collective preconception surrounding the sport. They created a hyperreal, Disney-esque facade of a clubhouse and placed it inside the Headhouse. This facade, which is met by driving through a lantern-lit turnaround, features a covered portico, bay-windows, clapboarding, and a shingled roof. The instant country club ambience functions as a physical and psychological threshold to the Golf Club at Pier 59. The architects clearly wanted to provide an experience that would take visitors to a distant place, far away from the concerns of the city just a few hundred yards away.

The Butler Rogers Baskett architects orchestrated a Golf Club on Pier 59 that beyond providing a relaxing getaway, is the country's most technologically advanced golf driving range and teaching center.

The Golf Club features an automatic tee-up system, 52 weather-protected hitting stalls on four floors, and a 200-yard fairway with target greens . Unlike the other piers, the driving range has no roof, and to keep 60,000 balls from flying off the 120 by 585 foot platform, the architects enclosed the entire fairway with 190,000 square feet of netting.

The design and installation of the netting, which had to be supported by 12, 150-foot-tall freestanding steel towers, created one of the biggest challenges that the architects faced during construction.

Structural engineers, Thornton-Tomasetti, determined that the only way the two-foot-thick, concrete-slab pier could take the load was through a series of six steel piles driven into the Hudson River to support each of the twelve towers. In some cases, these piles were driven nearly 250 feet before reaching bedrock.

The architects incorporated a highly advanced, sensor-controlled Japanese system that automatically lowers the nets and thus closes the driving range during high winds, snow, or freezing rain. The Butler Rogers Baskett team were the first architects to incorporate and build such a structure in the U.S., and the first anywhere to use such a structure on a pier.

Once inside the 10,000-square-foot clubhouse, one is greeted with black and white photographs of some of golf's most famous players. The clubhouse features both men's and women's locker rooms (for members only); bag storage for 200 bags; an 1,800-square-foot pro shop and the Ryder Cup Room for corporate and private events.

Once within one of the heated "outdoor" stalls one has a breathtaking view of the 1,500-square-foot synthetic putting green, the Hudson River and the New Jersey shore beyond.

The architects installed the first nylon synthetic turf landing area used in the United States.

Under the turf, the architects, working together with U.S. Indoor Turf, placed a one-inch-thick rubber padding which was recycled from old tires and poured and molded on site.

The turf and rubber were incorporated to provide a realistic bounce. The Golf Club also features a fully automatic ball delivery system designed and installed by Sunaga-Kaihatsu of Japan. The system transports balls mechanically via a vertical conveyor to the fourth tier.

From there, the balls are distributed horizontally via a belt conveyer and fed down rubber tubes to a ball stock box.

From the stock box to the tee there is a two-inch-diameter metal pipe under the concrete floor that delivers the ball to a mechanical tee device, which re-tees a ball every time one is hit or removed from the tee. Each of the 52 tee stalls is serviced by an automatic tee-up device which operate with prepaid mag-stripe cards that activate the tee through a console at each tee station.

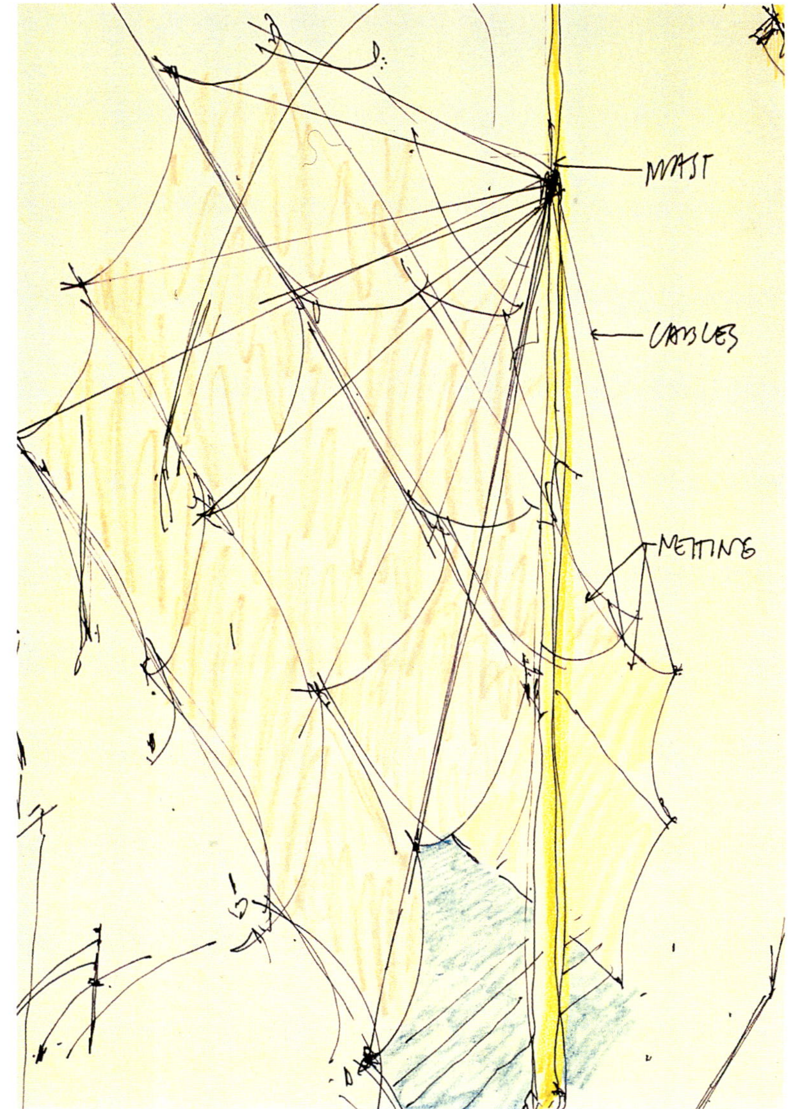

Each golfer can adjust his or her tee height, and the stalls are also equipped with call buttons to the front desk if any problems should arise.

The Golf Club at Pier 59 is the result of the creative integration of pier technology and modern optimized lightweight structural towers. It is also a surprisingly unexpected architectural experience.

The Butler Rogers Baskett architects established a complex architectural language that works within the dichotomy established between the vernacular and the high-tech, the predictable and the unexpected, to create a place that is truly unique.

View of Clubhouse
facade at Chelsea Piers
Golf Club during final
stages of construction.
Below, rendering
of Chelsea Piers Golf
Club entrance facade
and rendering of driving
range landing platform
showing natural
vegetation typical of
the New York harbor
and waterfront.

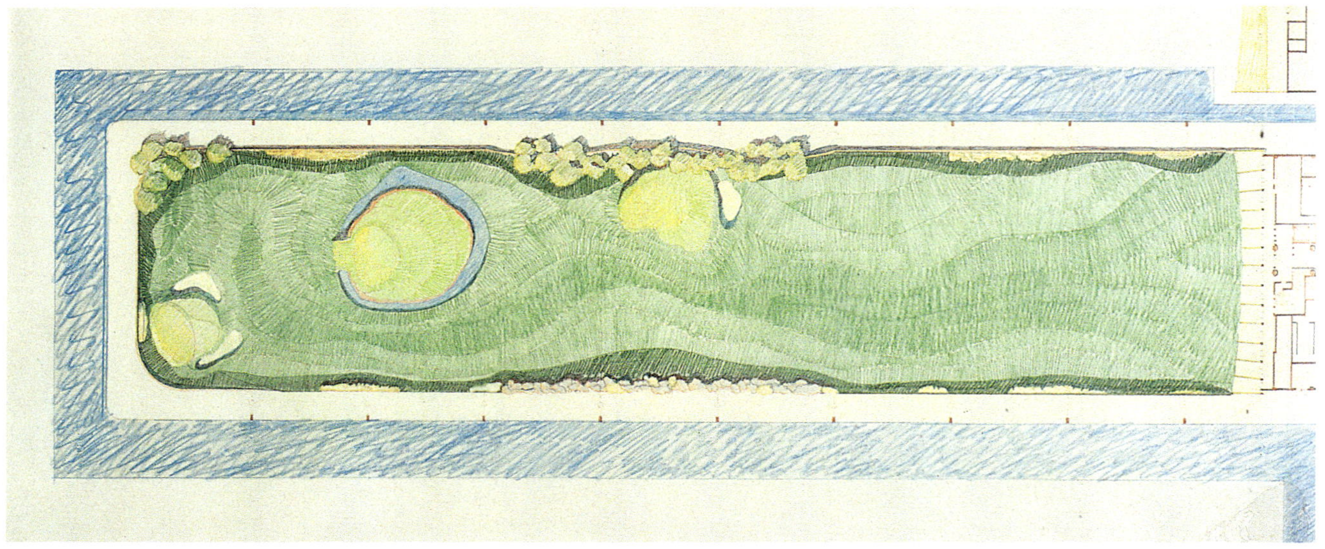

View of the Clubhouse
which serves as entrance
to the Chelsea Piers Golf
Club located within
the Chelsea Pier's
Headhouse complete
with 9-hole putting
green.

A look at the hitting stalls form the northern side of Pier 59. The stalls are weather-protected and can be used year-round. Note the space heaters hanging from the ceiling.

Early evening on the
driving range at the
Chelsea Piers Golf Club
with netting system
being raised.
Below, view of Chelsea
Piers Golf Club driving
range from hitting stall
on second tier.

Previous page, view of 52-stall golf driving range from the end of Pier 59 looking east.

View of pier 59 at sunset with man on private boat. Below, view of Pier 59 at sunset.

Pier 59 during early
stages of project. Images
show slab of pier as
connected to Headhouse.

View of hitting stalls
at the Chelsea Piers Golf
Club as seen from
the public esplanade.

The Chelsea Piers Golf
Club as seen from Pier 60.

Opposite page, view of
Chelsea Piers Golf Club
hitting stalls through
netting and the Chelsea
Piers Marina structure as
seen from the Hudson
River.

SURFSIDE 3